I May Not Be An Expert, But I Do Know This...

Tassy Tassel

All Around Publishing, Inc.
www.allaroundpublishinginc.com

> Warning: The reproduction and sale of this book without authorization is illegal. All rights reserved: No part of this book may be reproduced or transmitted in any means or in any form without written permission from the publisher.

I May Not Be An Expert, But I Do Know This…
Copyright © 2020 by Tassy Tassel

First Publication Date: March 2021

Cover art by Zequeatta Jaques
All art and logo copyright © 2020 by All Around Publishing, Inc.

ISBN: 978-1-7344314-1-4

Publisher
All Around Publishing, Inc.

This book is a great read for young adults and older adults alike.
The staff of All Around Publishing, Inc.

This is a journal of random wisdom, random observation, and random advice. You may like it, you may not. *Tassy Tassel*

DEDICATION

Special thanks to the people who have come in and out of my life (good and bad), and some, who were on the sidelines and didn't even know I was aware of you; you all made me grow as an individual. Each one of you caused me to reflect on life, to question things, and as a result, you made me wiser.

I May Not Be An Expert,
But I Do Know This...

Tassy Tassel

I May Not Be An Expert, But I Do Know This...

People will *look* you in the *eye* and lie *straight* to your *face*.

There are good people and there are bad, the bad might win for a short spell but eventually they do lose.

I May Not Be An Expert, But I Do Know This...

Not all *family* members will have *your* back. Some wield the *knife*.

Family members are chosen for you; however, you can choose to disengage.

I May Not Be An Expert, But I Do Know This...

If your spouse *cheats* once, shame on him/her. If your spouse *cheats* twice, *divorce* the loser. You have a serial *cheater*.

Deceive me once shame on you, deceive again, and allowed to get away with it, shame on me.

I May Not Be An Expert, But I Do Know This...

When you *wake* in the morning with a *bad* attitude the *whole day* turns bad.

You set the tone for your life, not anyone else.

I May Not Be An Expert, But I Do Know This...

Fact memorization and test taking skills are good while in school or college, just don't equate them to someone *having common sense* or real-life *intelligence*.

An ability to adapt to different environments is a must for everyday living.

I May Not Be An Expert, But I Do Know This...

When *play wrestling* with your husband, you can take him down in one beautiful swoop by grabbing the bottom hems of his jean-covered legs and *giving* a quick yank.

Be ready to run, because you will be next.

I May Not Be An Expert, But I Do Know This...

Some people age like a fine wine, others more like *clabbered* milk!

Be the fine wine. Attitude. Attitude. Attitude.

I May Not Be An Expert, But I Do Know This...

Housework is more *manageable* when put on a schedule.

Every day...Keep kitchen clean
Monday........................Vacuum, Dust, Do a couple of loads of laundry
Tuesday...Clean mirrors, Sweep floors
Wednesday....................... Clean bathrooms, Strip beds and change linens, Do a couple of loads of laundry
Thursday..Sweep floors, Mop floors
Friday............... Do a couple of loads of laundry, Clean out refrigerator
Saturday ....Clean bathrooms, Wash floor rugs
Sunday...No housework—Do something fun

I May Not Be An Expert, But I Do Know This...

If a *friend* or a *family member* comes to you and informs you that someone was gossiping about you, don't ask what was said—what you should question is this—Why did that someone feel comfortable talking about you in *their* presence?

Hmm....

I May Not Be An Expert, But I Do Know This...

Don't put off for *tomorrow* what you can do today.

Even small jobs loom large when delayed.

I May Not Be An Expert, But I Do Know This…

Don't *comment* on a matter unless you *know*—that you *know*—what you *know*.

Misinformation is not nice.

I May Not Be An Expert, But I Do Know This...

Vegetables are good for you but *candy* tastes better.

Don't let a weakness lead, what seems sweeter in the immediate is in the long haul usually bad for you.

I May Not Be An Expert, But I Do Know This...

If you have a *great idea* in the middle of the night, get up immediately and write it down.

My epiphany, why, oh why do you forsake me within the light of day?

I May Not Be An Expert, But I Do Know This...

It pays to *stop* and *think* about an issue before you rush in.

A moment of hesitation is not a bad thing.

I May Not Be An Expert, But I Do Know This...

No one *owns* another. If you are threatened by someone's attention to your significant other, the *problem* lies within you.

Work on that self-esteem.

I May Not Be An Expert, But I Do Know This...

Your *thoughts* direct your life so be careful your *thoughts*.

Negativity will battle within to gain the upper hand. Fight it. Change a negative thought immediately to a positive direction.

I May Not Be An Expert, But I Do Know This...

If you have a *secret* and you want few to know it, how many people do you tell? *Zero! Zilch!*

Keep your mouth closed.

I May Not Be An Expert, But I Do Know This...

Every second of your *life* counts. Live your moments or they are lost.

Don't live in the past and don't live for the future, live in and for today.

I May Not Be An Expert, But I Do Know This...

I believe that *God* wants to bless us, but that we, *ourselves*, block most of those blessings.

Don't prevent your blessings! Give praise to God regardless of any current situation and obey his Ten Commandments.

I May Not Be An Expert, But I Do Know This...

When on your knees working the ground under a rose bush, and you look up, and are *eye ball* to *eye ball* with a snake, you *can* do an acrobatic back flip and swim backwards on top of the ground!

Your heart may take a moment to quiet down.

I May Not Be An Expert, But I Do Know This...

Others perception of you is *their* reality not yours.

Put your best foot forward and don't worry about what others think of you.

I May Not Be An Expert, But I Do Know This...

Some days a marriage is all *kissy, kissy*, and other days, when meeting in the hallway of your home, your hair stands up on the back of your neck and you face off from each other like two stray alley cats fighting for pissing territory.

All marriages have good and bad days don't give up on yours too easily.

I May Not Be An Expert, But I Do Know This...

You are not as *dumb* as you think you are, but you're not as *smart* either!

Keep Learning.

I May Not Be An Expert, But I Do Know This...

Don't expect others to make you *happy*, find that *happiness* yourself.

Invest in you.

I May Not Be An Expert, But I Do Know This...

I believe in a *Heaven* and a *hell* and I believe that *God* wants the best for us all.

It is good to read the Bible.

I May Not Be An Expert, But I Do Know This…

Your body is a *living*, breathing machine.
It must be thoughtfully cared for or it breaks down.

A healthy body requires a healthy life!

I May Not Be An Expert, But I Do Know This...

Tattoos like a *drug* are addictive.

Watch yourself.

I May Not Be An Expert, But I Do Know This...

Expect *goodness* in others, but don't have a blind eye.

When your intuition sounds an alarm bell, listen.

I May Not Be An Expert, But I Do Know This...

Life is not *easy*. Some days you want to hide and hate the world. *Don't.*

A private prayer each morning relieves pain.

I May Not Be An Expert, But I Do Know This...

You should *live* in the moment, but you must also be *studious* as to your future.

All your actions in your today's builds your tomorrow's.

I May Not Be An Expert, But I Do Know This...

You should *smile* more often; your life will be *better* for it if you do.

A smile on the outside works its way to the inside.

I May Not Be An Expert, But I Do Know This...

Remove your shoes occasionally and walk barefoot in the grass. It is good for the *mind*, *body*, and *spirit*.

Listen to the birds sing while you are at it.

I May Not Be An Expert, But I Do Know This...

It is your *responsibility* to make sure that your child is safe, secure, and feels loved.

Morals matter.

I May Not Be An Expert, But I Do Know This...

When you *stub* your big toe on a doorframe within your home, in the middle of the night, a well-placed curse word *does* help to relieve the pain!

Just don't use God's name in vain.

I May Not Be An Expert, But I Do Know This...

I believe there is an *evil* force and a *Good* force in the universe, and both are vying for our souls.

Think long and hard as to which force it is you choose to follow.

I May Not Be An Expert, But I Do Know This...

Some people display a high *arrogance* as to their skill set in something, however, when checked out, it is not so great.

Keep your nose out of the air and keep learning.

I May Not Be An Expert, But I Do Know This...

To read a *book* is a mini vacation from everyday *life*.

Read daily.

I May Not Be An Expert, But I Do Know This...

You can be *too* nice!

If someone intentionally disrespects you, put a stop to it instantly. If it is someone who works for someone else, talk to his or her supervisor. If it's a stranger on the street, leave the situation. If it is a friend or family member, let them know their behavior is unacceptable, and if they continue, distance yourself from them, remove them from within your life circle.

I May Not Be An Expert, But I Do Know This...

Most *weight* gain is due to a bending *elbow*.

If you have no (genuine) medical reason for your weight, take a look at that weak elbow.

I May Not Be An Expert, But I Do Know This...

When your dog *disrupts* a wasp nest and a horde of angry wasps' swarm, you learn how to breakdance in an *instant*!

Screaming is optional.

I May Not Be An Expert, But I Do Know This...

There is a *difference* between not caring what others think about you and just being *unkind*.

Rudeness is rudeness no matter how it's sliced.

I May Not Be An Expert, But I Do Know This...

It is best to *limit* your *television* watching.

Not all things broadcasted are good for you or truthful.

I May Not Be An Expert, But I Do Know This...

A man or woman *should not* bad mouth their spouse to others.

Build up don't tear down.

I May Not Be An Expert, But I Do Know This...

It is your *responsibility* that your child knows right from wrong; teach him/her the 10 Commandments from the Bible.

Morals matter.

I May Not Be An Expert, But I Do Know This...

Make *time* for your spouse. A relationship stays strong when you seek each other out.

A good marriage takes effort.

I May Not Be An Expert, But I Do Know This...

If you run with *trash,* you become *trash.*

Be careful your friends.

I May Not Be An Expert, But I Do Know This...

If you *need* a job, don't declare that you *won't* work for less than this pay or this position, and then proceed to live off someone who works any job at any pay to cover the bills!

Bum! Get a job!

I May Not Be An Expert, But I Do Know This...

Time marches by for everyone! How sad it will be at your life-end to realize you only *existed*!

Live your life! Try new things! Stretch those dreams!

I May Not Be An Expert, But I Do Know This...

Children are *precious* jewels.

If you (man or woman) don't believe this as truth, don't reproduce! Go to a doctor and make your non-reproduction permanent!

I May Not Be An Expert, But I Do Know This...

You are not *too good* to buy second-hand!

Many great bargains are found and money saved by buying used.

I May Not Be An Expert, But I Do Know This...

A day at the *beach*, a *walk*, time together as a family is more precious than diamonds flashed on a finger.

Give the gift of yourself. You won't regret it.

I May Not Be An Expert, But I Do Know This...

Have *principles* and *stand* by them.

If you don't think for yourself, someone else will do it for you.

I May Not Be An Expert, But I Do Know This...

You need to give yourself some alone time.
Take at least ten minutes a day to *reflect* on life.

Yes, it's a good thing.

I May Not Be An Expert, But I Do Know This...

If you want to fight *crime*, you should begin to teach the *10 Commandments* listed in the Bible to your children from the moment of their birth.

Exodus 20:2 – 17
Deuteronomy 5:6 – 21

I May Not Be An Expert, But I Do Know This...

Money is *not* evil. It is an *inanimate* object.

What some people do for the love of money now that can be evil! Yikes!

I May Not Be An Expert, But I Do Know This…

In the *spring*, how great a feeling it is to open your house windows and let that fresh air flow thru-out your home.

Unless your allergies are acting up, and then you should know better!

I May Not Be An Expert, But I Do Know This...

It is *odd* how someone can claim that he/she doesn't believe in God and then get so *irate* with others who do.

~~Hmm....~~ Let's think about this. Why so enraged if you don't believe? Company required, I guess, if wrong?

I May Not Be An Expert, But I Do Know This...

Your perception of age will determine your *old agedness* not your actual calendar *age*.

Eat healthy, exercise, and keep note of that attitude.

I May Not Be An Expert, But I Do Know This…

Self-doubt kills more dreams than anything.

Try, try and try again.

I May Not Be An Expert, But I Do Know This...

Never accept *anything* at face value.

If 9 out of 10 people prefer something—always check to see who paid for the study. Is it the person selling?

I May Not Be An Expert, But I Do Know This...

It is said that you should *talk* to your plants and they will grow better.

Therefore, with this in mind, when fertilizing and tending to your plants, softly and lovingly state, "If you don't do well this year, I'm going to rip your ass out and throw you in the burn pile."

Reach out and touch a few as you speak. You know to let them know that you care. Keep in mind, this technique may not always work.

I May Not Be An Expert, But I Do Know This...

Don't let your *past* dictate your future.

When the sun comes up each morning, it's a new day and a new beginning.

I May Not Be An Expert, But I Do Know This...

There are people who can *sell* a rock and say it's a pet.

It has happened.
Take a moment and let that sink in.

I May Not Be An Expert, But I Do Know This...

If you are in a *position* where a child sees you as an authority figure and you act maliciously, you are a *low* life.

A schoolteacher told a first-grade student that she couldn't read. This child read her grade level just fine, but after the teacher stated she couldn't read, the child refused to open another book. She would cry and say, "No, my teacher says I can't read." Only upon transferring this child to another school and a new teacher informing her that she could read did she bounce back.

Yes, a "teacher" really did this.

I May Not Be An Expert, But I Do Know This...

Debt is easy, getting out from under it is *not*!

The thrill of possession wears thin with each required payment.

I May Not Be An Expert, But I Do Know This...

Not everyone will *support* your dreams, so be careful who you listen to when receiving advice. Don't let others derail you with their negativity.

Remember, if you try something and it doesn't work out at least you tried!

I May Not Be An Expert, But I Do Know This...

I have *always* learned more from my mistakes than from my successes.

Suck it up, crybaby. You will survive this.

I May Not Be An Expert, But I Do Know This...

It's okay to have a lazy day *once in a while*, just don't make a *habit* of it.

Inaction can lead to a lifetime of inertia.

I May Not Be An Expert, But I Do Know This...

Oh, how we love to make known the *flaws of others,* while unable to see our own.

Recognize your own shortcomings and you won't be so swift to slice away with that evil tongue.

I May Not Be An Expert, But I Do Know This...

Don't let *past* mistakes damage your future self.

With each new rising of the sun, you have an opportunity for a new beginning. Use it.

I May Not Be An Expert, But I Do Know This...

If your answer to failure is to *blame* others for it, you will *never* move forward.

Look inward and seek an understanding of self.

I May Not Be An Expert, But I Do Know This...

To *experience* life you must live it!

Watch a sunrise: Observe a sunset: Laugh: Cry: Lose loved ones: Find loved ones: On and on we go, that is life!

I May Not Be An Expert, But I Do Know This...

Do not embrace *bitterness* toward another.

Forgiveness relieves a heavy burden.

I May Not Be An Expert, But I Do Know This...

Life is *not* fair and it never will be.

Good and bad days go hand-in-hand with daily living.
We may not understand the bad days, but it is what it is.
Your mindset will determine if the bad days win.

I May Not Be An Expert, But I Do Know This...

No one is born *proficient* in anything; you become skilled at something by studying it, working at it, and never ever giving up.

Put forth some effort!

I May Not Be An Expert, But I Do Know This...

You *can't* force change in anyone; a person must want transformation.

It's hard to watch someone self-destruct, but we choose our life path.

I May Not Be An Expert, But I Do Know This...

What you *expect* out of life is usually what you get.

Have a high aim.

I May Not Be An Expert, But I Do Know This...

To explode with anger is *easy* but not always wise.

Practice self-control, you will be better for it health wise and relationship wise.

I May Not Be An Expert, But I Do Know This...

A *clean* house is restful.

Yes, I'm talking about your physical home, but this can go for your psyche also.

I May Not Be An Expert, But I Do Know This…

You should strive to be *happy* for others when they succeed.

Envy is a poison that destroys the carrier.

I May Not Be An Expert, But I Do Know This...

Be *polite* even when you don't feel like it.

What you feed grows and circles back to you.

I May Not Be An Expert, But I Do Know This...

A *journey* can only begin with movement.

Don't let fear shackle your dreams.

I May Not Be An Expert, But I Do Know This...

With *any* job that you have, do it to the best of your *ability*!

Each experience in life prepares you for the next step.

I May Not Be An Expert, But I Do Know This...

As a*n adult* you should know that when you leave *home* and venture out into the big, wide world, don't expect a pat on the back or a high-five from others just because you pooped.

Stand tall, keep your shoulders thrown back, prove your worth, and remember, the outside world is not your mother!

I May Not Be An Expert, But I Do Know This...

It is okay to be *sad*—just don't pull up a chair and invite it to sit down and stay.

Sadness is a part of the life experience.
It will eventually fade if you allow it to.

I May Not Be An Expert, But I Do Know This...

You are the *only* one who will live your life!

Be kind, be thoughtful, but always be you!

I May Not Be An Expert, But I Do Know This…

If always on the lookout for an *insult,* be assured, you will find it.

Get that chip off your shoulder.

I May Not Be An Expert, But I Do Know This...

Don't compare your life to what others project.

Private lives may not be so great.

I May Not Be An Expert, But I Do Know This...

Early morning rising allows a person time to think, to wonder, and to talk with God.

Seek Him out.

I May Not Be An Expert, But I Do Know This...

Be *careful* your words—what you say you draw toward you.

Watch that verbal chitchat.

I May Not Be An Expert, But I Do Know This...

If you make a daily habit to *count* your blessings, you won't have time for the *woe is me*, to take over your mind.

Even a miniscule thing can be counted as a blessing.
✔ I have coffee this morning.

I May Not Be An Expert, But I Do Know This...

You should say this daily:
It's a beautiful *day*! It's a beautiful *world*!

Your life experience is what you make it.

I May Not Be An Expert, But I Do Know This...

1. Do not have other gods before God.
2. Do not make or worship graven images.
3. Do not take God's name in vain.
4. Know the Sabbath day and keep the Sabbath day holy.
5. Honor your parents.
6. Don't murder anyone.
7. Don't commit adultery.
8. Don't steal.
9. Don't lie about others.
10. Don't covet what others have.

The 10 Commandments from the Bible as I memorized them.

The End

About The Author

Tassy Tassel lives in the U.S. and enjoys many activities (hiking, gardening, writing, reading, and even exercising at the gym (yes, (exercising) hard to believe isn't it). She has a Masters in Applied Psychology and enjoys life. She and her husband have two children and four grandchildren—the children and grandchildren, of course, are a source of pride.

All Around Publishing, Inc.
www.allaroundpublishinginc.com

www.ingramcontent.com/pod-product-compliance
Lightning Source LLC
Chambersburg PA
CBHW042026100526
44587CB00029B/4318